COMMUNICATION:
From Cave Writing to Television

to Zachary moench:

by the same author

A CAP FOR MUL CHAND

TIM AND THE PURPLE WHISTLE

SEA LADY

SUPERSTITIOUS? HERE'S WHY!
(with Claudia de Lys)

COMMUNICATION:

From Cave Writing to Television

JULIE FORSYTH BATCHELOR

Illustrated by C. D. Batchelor

HARCOURT, BRACE & WORLD, INC., NEW YORK

384

COPYRIGHT, 1953, BY

JULIE FORSYTH BATCHELOR

J.9.61

LIBRARY OF CONGRESS CATALOG CARD NUMBER: 53-7860

PRINTED IN THE UNITED STATES OF AMERICA

Contents

CONTENTS

COMMUNICATION:
From Cave Writing to Television

CHAPTER ONE

The Way Communication Began

TALKING and listening are simple things you do every day. Yet these are two of the most important things in your life. For by talking you tell other people your thoughts, and by listening you learn theirs. We call this communication.

Talking to others can be done by: spoken words, written words, and signals. Listening is done with your ears. But if you are deaf you can listen with your eyes. If you are both deaf and blind you must listen with your fingers.

Children who are blind read by running their fingers over pages that have raised letters. This kind of printing is called Braille.

Book in Braille

Some children who are unable to speak can talk by using a finger language.

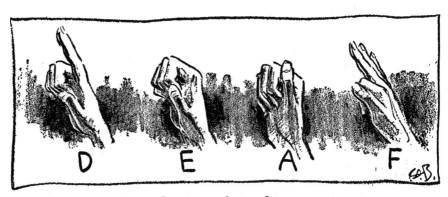

Four letters in finger language

Today there are many, many kinds of communication. It's fun to see the number you can name.

4

Here are six ways messages are seen. What are they?

Here are six ways messages are heard:

These riddles will add six more ways of communication to your list. Or seven, if you guess two right answers to the first riddle.

1. What is it that has pictures and talking at the same time?
2. What is it that awakens you in time for school?
3. What is it that a policeman blows as a signal?
4. What is it that warns ships when there's a fog?
5. What is it that tells when a fire engine is coming?
6. What is it that tells drivers they are coming to a school?

Now you know at least eighteen ways of communicating with others. If you have a bulletin board put a picture of each kind on it. Or paste them in a scrapbook. Pictures you can't find you can draw.

If you haven't a bulletin board you can make one from a large piece of heavy cardboard, cork, or soft wood. Paste or nail a narrow frame around it if you wish. Use thumbtacks for hanging your pictures.

You've heard of most of these ways of communication since you were small. But way back in the early days, when your great, great (and many more greats) grandmothers and grandfathers lived, no one knew *any* of these ways. So you can imagine how different life was then.

In those days you'd have lived in a cave or up in high rocks called cliffs. As a caveman's child you'd have spoken only in growls or grunts or screams. For there weren't any words and there weren't any languages. If you wanted to tell someone something you'd just have to act it out.

Suppose Mr. Caveman who lived next door shook his heavy club at you. Would you think he was pleased with you? What would he be telling you if he danced about happily as he pretended to eat birds' eggs? What would you do if he growled like a bear and waved for you to run away with him?

Today we still use some sign language. You lift your hand when you say "Hi!"; wave it when saying good-by; shake your fist to show you're angry; and shrug your shoulders when you don't know the answer.

What word does a policeman mean when he holds up one hand? What does your mother mean when she shakes her head from side to side?

You've seen the umpire at a baseball game use these signals to tell everyone what has happened:

Suppose a boy who didn't speak English moved next door. How could you tell him in sign language, "Let's play catch"; or, "Come over and eat lunch at my house"?

You still sometimes grunt as the caveman did. That's when you say "Uh huh" for yes, and "Mmmm" when you smell something good to eat. What other sounds do you make that stand for words?

Since Mr. Caveman didn't use words he wasn't interested in writing as we know it. But he drew animals on the walls of his cave. Perhaps he drew them for fun. But we believe he made them as a record of ones he'd seen or killed.

These animals weren't the dog, cat and horse you know so well. Mr. Caveman drew animals important at that time —the deer, the buffalo, and the mammoth. This last animal doesn't live now. It was a huge elephant that often stood nine feet high. Today we speak of very large things as being mammoth.

The earliest caveman drew stiff-looking animals with only two legs—like the kind you drew when you were younger. Later cavemen made animals with four legs and in color.

What do you suppose Mr. Caveman drew with—for of course there were no pencils, crayons or paint brushes? Sometimes he used sharp stones to cut pictures on the rock walls of his cave. Or he worked with burnt wood called charcoal, which is still used by artists. Colored paint was made from colored clays and from plants.

We know about these drawings of thousands of years ago because some are still on the walls of caves where the cavemen lived. Other such paintings have been placed in city museums, so that many people can see them.

You might enjoy having your own museum. It can be a shelf or two in your room. Keep there the things you make and collect about communication. Be sure and label everything. If you know the date when an article was used write that on the label.

As the years went by people began to write picture messages. Our American Indians still used picture writing when the first settlers came. They wrote on bark and on the skins of wild animals. These skins were dried and stretched on frames. Often picture writing was done on the outside of wigwams which were made from animal hides. Here are some of the pictures they used:

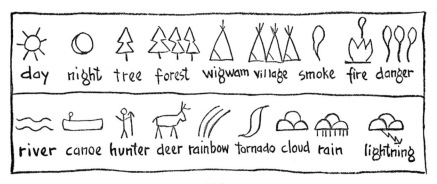

day   night   tree   forest   wigwam   village   smoke   fire   danger

river   canoe   hunter   deer   rainbow   tornado   cloud   rain   lightning

What message is this Indian writing? Read from the bottom up.

As more words came to be spoken these were put into sentences. Then people understood each other better.

When you were a baby you learned words such as *dog, cat, see*. Later you put them into the sentence, "See the dog and cat." That's what those early people did. Only it took them much longer to put words into sentences—thousands

11

of years longer.

For awhile people were satisfied to draw pictures for words. But some words like *how, are* and *then* can't be drawn. An alphabet of many letters was needed. So finally the letters we use today were formed. The story of the alphabet is a long, interesting one. You might like to read it in the encyclopedia.

The earliest alphabet had 22 letters. How many does our alphabet have?

Letters made writing much easier. However, the Chinese never stopped using a form of picture writing. Signs or symbols still stand for their words and sentences. Here are some of them:

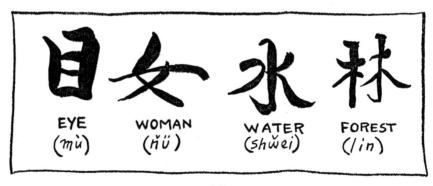

EYE
(mù)

WOMAN
(nü)

WATER
(shwei)

FOREST
(lin)

We use signs for certain of our words today. Do you know these:

$$+ \quad - \quad = \quad \times \quad \div \quad \cent \quad \$ \quad \# \quad \&$$

Carpenters write these signs after numbers: ' to stand for feet, and " to stand for inches.

Since each country made up its own words each had a different language. Today, there are over 2,000 languages in use. You probably think English is spoken by the most people. But more speak Chinese than any other language.

You're very lucky if someone at your house knows a foreign language. Be sure to learn it, for it's easier to learn at home where you can practice often. Besides, knowing another language makes you a more interesting person, and helps you to understand others. Some people can speak three or four languages.

How do you suppose Mr. Caveman counted? On his fingers and toes, of course. When he needed more than twenty he used sticks or stones.

If you use your fingers when you add or subtract you're like the caveman. And he wasn't very smart!

Even after people could write words, they sometimes still liked to use some pictures. We call this rebus. The pictures or numbers used may stand for the sound of the word, or for the word itself. Here's the way it's done.

One picture:

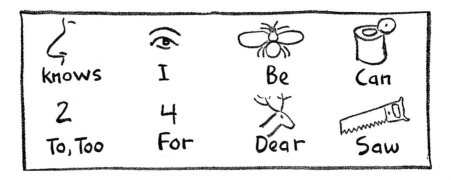

knows	I	Be	Can
2	4	Dear	Saw
To, Too	For		

Two pictures:

| Before | Hilltop | Caveman |
| Lighthouse | Mail man | Crowbar |

Picture and part of word written out:

4 -get ✐-er t-👤 n-👂
Forget Corner There Near

b-💍 b-👁 🔑-p base-💍
Bring Buy. By Keep Baseball

Now turn to page 109 and see if you can read the rebus letter there. If you can, you're ready to write rebus letters and stories of your own.

How did you learn to talk as a baby? You learned by copying the people you were with. So of course you spoke the language of those people. If when young you had been put in a home in Holland you'd have grown up speaking Dutch. And it would be as hard for you to learn English as it is for a Dutch youngster.

Down through the years more and better ways of communication were discovered. In learning how to tell others their thoughts and ideas, people became better thinkers.

15

In reading books they found out about other parts of the world.

Thus, better communication made people more civilized. This means they were less like wild animals. So you can see why talking and listening—those simple things you do each day—are so important.

CHAPTER TWO

In the Early Days:
Messages Seen, Heard, and Carried

WE LIKE to send messages quickly. The telegraph and wireless flash our words across the world in a few minutes. But in olden times, of course, people did not know about the telegraph and wireless.

Fire can be seen a long way off, especially at night. So signal fires were an early way of sending news quickly. Bonfires built on top of hills could be seen for many miles.

Each tribe had its own fire language. It was in code, which means that signs stand for words or sentences. This was the great-grandfather of our Morse code of today which we'll talk about in Chapter Five.

Here's how that early fire code worked. After the bonfire was burning well a man would kneel beside it. He'd cover the fire with a wet animal hide, then quickly uncover it. So many flashes of fire would mean certain words. Both short and long flashes were used.

If there was news that many towns should know, such as of a war being won, it was told by relay fires. Each village had a pile of wood ready on its highest hill. When the town nearest the fighting lighted its bonfire the next village would light its. And so on across the country until every town knew what had happened.

Later, high stone towers were built and bonfires were kept burning on top of them. These were called beacon lights.

The American Indians also used fire for signaling. They covered and uncovered their flames with damp bark. A long flame followed by a short flame might mean, "We're coming to visit you."

If the fire was uncovered quickly three times it said, "Danger is near."

The fastest signal was shooting a burning arrow into the sky. That meant DANGER or WAR!

In daylight, fires can't be seen far away. So the Indians

used a smoke signal. They built a small bonfire on a hill. Then they partly covered it with wet grass or leaves so more smoke would rise into the air. Two Indians held a blanket over the flames. By quickly pulling away the blanket they'd send up puffs of smoke that could be seen far away. There were big and little puffs, depending on how long the blanket was held up. Each tribe had its own smoke code.

Many beacon lights were built on the rocky shores of lakes, rivers and oceans to warn ships of danger. These were the first lighthouses. Fires from large oak logs made the first lights. After coal was discovered it was used because it burned longer.

The first lighthouses in America were lighted by many candles. Later, oil lamps, which gave a better light, were used.

Today, lighthouses have lamps lighted by gas or electricity. Each lamp has a glass lens that revolves around a strong light. Parts of the lens are covered, so as it turns light shows in flashes. Most big lighthouses have their own signals—a certain number of flashes. That way sailors know which lighthouse they're watching. The lighthouse at Scituate, Massachusetts, blinks its light like this:

— ———— ———. Someone said that was the number of letters in the sentence "I love you." Now sailors always call it the "I Love You" lighthouse.

Did you know that most lighthouses have a fog signal? You may have heard the deep call of the foghorn. And many lighthouses have radio signals to help ships in very bad weather when sailors can't see the light or hear the foghorn.

Sometimes, out from shore where it might not be easy to build a lighthouse, a steel ship is anchored. This is called a lightship. It stays in one place all the time with several men aboard. It has a lamp, foghorn, and radio signals. Also the lightship has warning bells.

Fire is dangerous and it's red in color, so since early days the color red has been used to say "Danger." You've seen red lanterns near broken sidewalks and holes in roads. Automobile tail lights are red.

Look for the red light near the word EXIT when you're at the movie house or inside other large buildings. That word tells you, "This way out if there's a fire!" What word does a traffic light mean when it turns red? Where else have you seen a red light that either says "Stop" or "Danger"?

When you shout at a friend several blocks away you're using the first kind of communication to be heard—the voice. But early men wanted messages to be heard much farther than voices can travel. They did this by using something that was hollow inside.

Fishermen living near the seashore found big conch shells to blow into. Shepherds used rams' horns to call their sheep together.

Conch Shell   Ram's Horn

Those high stone towers built for beacon lights were a help in sending the voice a far distance. Men stood at the top and shouted from tower to tower through a megaphone. You've seen a cheer leader's megaphone. These early people used one like it only it was made from skins of animals.

Drums, or tom-toms, were another means of sending

messages far off. Trunks of trees made fine tom-toms. These were hollowed out and skins of animals pulled tightly over one or both ends. Each tribe had its own drum language. Slow and long taps stood for certain words and sentences.

To send messages to many far-off villages a telegraph drum was set up. This large drum was partly buried in the ground, for sound travels better underground. A telegraph tom-tom could be heard ten or twelve miles away.

As the drummer in the nearest settlement heard the first sounds he'd start tapping the message on his drum for the next village. And so on from village to village, just like those relay bonfires.

Even today African natives use these same kinds of

drums. It's much quicker than sending a runner through the jungle.

You and a friend might like to tap out messages to each other. You can sit in different rooms and tap softly. Make up your own code, or use the Morse code on page 112.

Some of the first bells we know about hung in churches. As bells do now, these rang on Sundays. Also, they rang whenever a baby was born, someone died, there was a fire, danger was near, or when a war was over. So you see how important bells were then.

Each of these early bells had a name such as Mary or John. Some of the most famous bells had nicknames. Today we still call two bells in London by their nicknames. Big Ben is the bell in the Westminster clock tower and Great Paul rings from St. Paul's Cathedral.

Your church may have bells called chimes. Music can be played on chimes, for these are made of several bells each with a different tone.

In days before street lights every town had a night watchman. He carried a bell and rang it every hour as he shouted the time and "All's clear." That meant all was safe.

It's fun to collect real bells for your museum. Or find pictures of each kind for your bulletin board or scrapbook. Here are some to look for:

Bells that say "Watch out" are on fire engines, trains, police cars, and ambulances.

Bells that say "Come here" are on schools, churches, ice cream carts, vegetable wagons, and doors of houses.

Bells that say "Here I am" are on cows, sheep and cats. In India camels and elephants wear them too.

Bells that tell time are on alarm clocks, ship's clocks, grandfather clocks, and clock towers.

Bells that say "DANGER" are on drawbridges, railroad crossings, and buoys.

These last—buoys—are floats that are anchored along channels to help ships stay in deep water. Or they may be near dangerous rocks. The first buoys were logs, kept in one place by a chain and anchor. Now they are made of steel and painted different colors. Each color tells sailors something special. For instance, a green buoy marks a sunken wreck of a ship.

While many buoys have bells, some have whistles. Do you know what makes their bells and whistles sound? It's the waves rocking the buoys.

Your school may have a fire bell code. Is it this one?

Many bells—Stop and listen
Two bells—Stand by your seat
Four bells—Walk from the building

The largest bell in the world is in Moscow, Russia. It weighs about 200 tons. While it was being cast a fire broke out which cracked it, so this bell was never rung. It's now on a stone platform. Forty children can stand inside it.

Our country's most important bell is the Liberty Bell. When the thirteen colonies declared their independence from England this great bell was rung. But now it is cracked so it will never ring again. You can see the Liberty Bell at Independence Hall in Philadelphia.

Whistles are important communication signals too. On the school playground a teacher often uses this code:

COMMUNICATION

One blow—Stop and listen
Two blows—Play
Three blows—Game is over

Trains have many whistle signals. When coming to a crossing they blow two long, a short, and another long blast. If a child or a cow is on the track the whistle blows many short toots.

Inside the train a communication cord runs through all the cars to the engine. You may have seen the cord pull that hangs beside each train door. If the conductor wants the train to stop at a station where it does not usually stop he pulls the cord three times. The engineer blows his whistle three short blasts, which means "O.K." If, when the train is stopped, the conductor wants the engine to back up he also pulls the cord three times. The engineer answers with three blasts.

Ships signal with whistles too. Here are three of them:

One short blast—I will pass to the right
Two short blasts—I will pass to the left
Three short blasts—I'm backing up

When one ship signals another, that ship repeats the signal. Then they know they understand each other. It's a good idea for you to repeat directions when you're sent on an errand. Besides finding out if you understand, it will help you to remember.

Today, libraries, schools and other buildings have flagpoles. But in the early days flags flew only from kings' palaces. A small, three-cornered flag, called a pennant, was carried by men in battle. Later, ships began using flags to send messages to each other.

Today, the captain of a ship has a code book of flag signals in all languages. So even if sailors on two ships don't speak the same language they can still talk in international flag code.

Have you seen U.S. Weather Bureau flags on the shores of the ocean or Great Lakes? By their colors these flags tell sailors and fishermen about the weather. A red flag with a black center means a bad storm is on the way. When you visit a weather bureau ask what the other colored flags mean.

A ship in distress may fly its flag upside down. That

means S O S or HELP!

Boy and Girl Scouts signal just as sailors do. Sometimes they use two flags, called semaphore signaling. Or they use one flag which is wigwag signaling, or wigwagging.

Wigwag signaling is easy to learn. You need a piece of cloth fastened to a stick. Orange cloth can be seen the farthest. Use the Morse code of dots and dashes on page 112.

Begin with the flag straight up. To make a dot, swing your flag to the right so the stick is even with your waist. For a dash, swing the flag to the left.

To end a word, swing your flag straight down toward your toes.

START   DOT   DASH   END

At night you can wigwag messages with a flashlight.

30

Swing it to the left and right just as you do the flag. To show the end of a message swing your flashlight up, then down.

From the beginning of spoken languages, messages have been carried by people. But news was often on the way for weeks and months, for most roads were rough paths through the forest, or there were no paths at all. The young men who could run the fastest carried the news.

Since the first people couldn't write, these runners had to learn the message by heart. They did this just as you do, by saying it over and over.

When news was carried a great distance runners ran in relays. These are like relay races at school. Every few miles a man would be waiting. When he'd heard the message he'd dash off to the next man.

In the very early days horses were only wild ponies and too small for men to ride on. But through the years they grew larger and people began riding them. Since a horse can travel faster than a man, messages were sent by horseback. This meant that better roads were needed.

One of the first carts used was a chariot. It was exciting

to drive, for it was built close to the ground with only two wheels, and could go very fast. Chariots often carried many letters, so these were the first mail cars.

Chariot

We don't think of birds carrying news. Yet the homing pigeon is one of our best messengers. When taken on a trip it knows the way home. Messages are put in tiny metal cases and fastened to a leg or under the wing.

The homing pigeon is usually gray in color. When it's a few months old men take it a short way from home and let it fly back. Then it's carried farther and farther away. When fully trained these pigeons can fly about 700 miles a day.

Runners who traveled where they might meet robbers

used to carry a basket of these pigeons. If captured they would open the door of the cage and let the birds fly home. Then other runners would be sent in their place.

Runner with homing pigeon

Today, people make a hobby of raising homing pigeons. During wars some birds are used by the Army for sending messages.

So through the years people have found many ways of communicating with each other.

Some men discovered one thing, other men other things. Very slowly, better and quicker ways of communication came to be used.

CHAPTER THREE

From Stone Tablets to Paper Books

FROM very early days down to the time that Columbus came to America, your ancestors—the people in your family before you—discovered many new things. The discoveries helping communication most were four important p's: paper, pens, pencils and the printing press.

For these four led to books, and books led to better-educated people. And of course, that meant a more civilized world.

Today we have so much paper that we forget about the time when no one had even heard of it. Remember those first early runners who had to learn their messages by heart? Well, even after news could be written the runner still had to memorize. For some of the first written messages were on stone. And that's heavy to carry!

We laugh as we imagine someone staggering along with a stone tablet under his arm. But stone was good for records in one way. The words could still be read thousands of years later.

Today, each large building has a stone at one of its corners telling the name of the building and the date it was built. Does your school have a cornerstone? If so, what is carved on it?

Some cornerstones are hollow. Records are placed inside. Then the stones are sealed. Hundreds of years later the records can be read.

Look for the cornerstone of your library and post office. The date may be in numbers used by the Romans, who lived in early Italy. You may know how to write Roman numerals. We use them often on clocks, in dates, and for chapters of books.

Since stone wasn't easy to carve people looked about for something better to write on. They found a clay which becomes hard when baked in the sun. This they formed into tablets. They made narrow, wedge-shaped marks on the soft clay. Then the clay was left out in the sun until solid. These tablets were fine if you didn't drop one!

You might like to make a clay tablet for your museum. Use modeling clay. Since this won't harden in the sun, press it flat on a thin board. Cut the end of a stick so it forms a flat triangle. Use this to press messages onto the clay. On the next page is an old clay tablet for you to copy.

When you label your tablet you can add the date. One clay tablet that has been found was used about 1450 B.C. That means 1,450 years *Before Christ* was born.

The Romans made something even better than a clay tablet to write on. This was a wax tablet. You know what a small slate looks like that children used in school many years ago. It had a narrow wooden frame around it. Well, wax tablets looked like that, with wax in place of the slate.

A stylus was used to indent letters in the wax. This tool was something like a nail file. One end was pointed to write with and the other was flat so you could smooth the wax if you made a mistake.

To make a wax tablet for your museum you'll need a thin board about six inches square. Nail or glue a narrow frame around this. Melt a dark-colored candle and fill the inside of the frame with wax. With a nail or file make marks deep enough for the board to show through.

A wax tablet book was made of several tablets fastened together by a piece of leather.

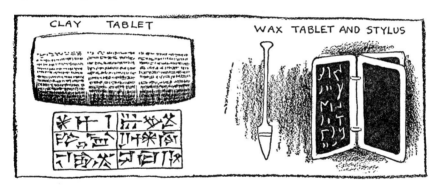

CLAY TABLET

WAX TABLET AND STYLUS

The Egyptians found out how to make a sort of paper which was still better to write on. Along their Nile River grew a plant called papyrus. They cut the inside of the stem of this plant, called pith, into many strips. These were laid side by side. More strips were placed on top, running the other way. A heavy weight pressed these two layers until their own juice or sap glued them together. When dry, the papyrus was rubbed with stones until it was smooth.

Instead of separate pages, papyrus was made in one piece. A piece long enough for a story or a letter was rolled on two sticks. This was called a scroll. To read it you held one stick in each hand. As you unrolled the scroll with one hand you rolled it up with the other. Imagine a class with each child reading from a scroll instead of a book!

A brush dipped in ink was used in writing on papyrus. The Egyptians wrote down the page in columns, starting from the right instead of from the left as we do. So each column had to be dry before another was started or the letters would be blurred.

Egyptian reading scroll

But ink in those days took a long time to dry. So what do you suppose they used for a blotter? Fine sand. It was kept in a little box and shaken out as salt is. If you didn't have sand you had to wave your scroll in the air after each column was penned.

Sand as a blotter was in use for hundreds of years. Sandbox shakers were used in this country by our early settlers.

It is difficult to get papyrus today although the plant still grows. But you can make a good example of a scroll out of drawing paper or a roll of white shelf paper. If you use drawing paper, paste the sheets side by side with the edges overlapping a little.

The handles of the scroll can be pieces of a broomstick. Cut them a little longer than your paper is wide. At each end of the handles fasten a wooden door stopper. Or carve the ends with a knife. Now paint these handles in gay colors.

Use glue or thumbtacks to fasten each end of your long strip of paper to the handles. Remember to do your columns with a brush and black ink. When the writing is dry roll the scroll up until the handles meet.

For a long time papyrus was the best writing material. But it couldn't be folded and only one side could be written on. Besides, this plant didn't grow in every country.

But sheep were raised almost everywhere. Remember how the early people used skins of wild animals on which to draw pictures? The skins of lambs and sheep are even better. They can be made into a sort of heavy paper called parchment. It's better than papyrus for it can be folded and both sides written on. Parchment was widely used for a long time.

If you get a piece of sheepskin or even a rabbit skin from your butcher you can make your own parchment. Turn to page 103 for the directions.

So you see, many years went by before paper was made. But meanwhile, people were using *the things they knew about.*

Before we begin the story of paper see how many different kinds you can find about your house. Get samples of each for your scrapbook or bulletin board. Here are some you may have: writing paper, drawing paper, wax paper, tissue paper, sandpaper, wallpaper, paper bag, paper napkin, cardboard, and a blotter.

Keep looking, for there are about 7,000 different kinds of paper in the world!

Have you ever seen a hornets' nest with its gray, paper-like covering? Hornets were the first papermakers. They use dried wood. This they mix with a liquid from their mouths. Then their jaws make this into a pulp. While the pulp is still wet it's formed into a nest.

Hornets leave their homes in the fall. If you find a nest you'll see what wonderful papermakers these insects are.

The First Papermaker

Man also uses dried wood for his paper. If you visit a

paper mill you'll see logs cut about five feet long. These are put into machines that chop them into chips. The chips are added to a chemical liquid. Then these are mixed until the wood is pulp.

Perhaps you've made pulp from old newspapers for masks and puppet heads. If you have, you know how easy it is to work with. In the mill, the woodpulp is placed between heavy presses while still wet and formed into sheets of paper.

Although most paper today is made from wood it can also be made from certain grasses, old paper, and cloth. The best writing paper is made from linen rags.

The first to make paper were the Chinese. They did this while people in other parts of the world were using papyrus and parchment. But travel wasn't easy then, so it was many years before others knew of their great discovery.

You remember how the Chinese have always used symbols for words instead of letters as we do. Since these symbols have both thin and wide lines, brushes are needed to write them. But people using the alphabet had to have something with a finer point. Thus pens came to be made.

A stiff reed was easy to find. The end was split up a little way so ink would stay on. Are some pen points split today?

A still better pen—called a quill pen—was made from the wing feathers of a goose, crow or turkey. The end of the feather was sharpened and also split. You can make one of these pens for your museum. Quill pens were used right up until steel pens were made. Fountain pen points are often made of gold.

Ink has been known for many years, for it was used on both papyrus and parchment. At first it was lampblack—the soot that smoke makes on pots and pans—mixed with glue. Even today lampblack is in printer's ink.

Some black ink we use now is made from gallnuts. These are lumps that form on trees where gallflies lay their eggs. You may find a gallnut, which looks like a ball, on the branch or leaf of an oak tree.

Spies sometimes use invisible ink so no one can read their writing. You can write a secret letter by using one of the following: lemon juice, onion juice, or milk. Whichever you use, have enough in a cup so the pen point will be half covered. Use a clean pen point to write with, and print your words carefully. When the paper is dry the words can't be seen. To read the message hold the paper near something hot, such as an electric light bulb, until the words appear.

Pencils at first were just pieces of lead. We still call them lead pencils, although that mineral is no longer actually used. Today, pencils are of graphite which is softer and makes a blacker mark.

When you buy pencils look for their numbers. A No. 1 pencil writes darker than a No. 2 pencil. In sharpening pencils, remember that turning the sharpener too fast breaks the points.

If you'd lived in the days before books you'd have said, "Tell me a story," perhaps oftener than you do today. Even grownups begged for stories then. Fathers and mothers told tales to their children. These later told the same stories to their children.

Do you suppose these stories were changed during the

years? You've probably played that game where someone whispers a sentence to the next person. He whispers it to the next person, and so on around the table. The last person says the sentence out loud. Very often it sounds quite different from the sentence you started out with. So it was with those early stories.

Men, known as minstrels, went from village to village telling and singing tales. Groups of actors did the same thing. They told stories by giving regular plays or shadow plays.

But eventually books came to be made of parchment. They were printed carefully by hand. Since small letters weren't used then, all stories were in capital letters.

These books were very beautiful. The first or initial letter of the first word on each page was drawn large and decorated. Around the margins were flowers and birds in lovely colors. Fine leather covered these books, and this was lettered in gold.

Ask your drawing teacher at school to show you how to make and decorate your initials.

Here are two initials and a part of a page from one of those old books (but without color).

Since these books took so long to finish they were very expensive. Only rich people could own them. Books became cheaper when paper was used. But they were still written by hand. A faster, better way of printing stories had to be found.

Here, the Chinese were first again. They used a block of wood the size of a page. On this they carved the words of the story. Then ink was brushed over this block and paper pressed upon it. This was called block printing. Many copies of the same page could be printed from one piece of wood.

Today we make bookmarks and Christmas cards the same way. On page 104 you'll find out how.

But still men wanted a faster way of making books. So many experiments were made. Finally, in several parts of the world, men discovered how to print by means of a printing press.

Each letter of the alphabet was cut out in metal. This was called type and the printer used it to spell out the words. He placed the words in a wooden frame, the size of a page. This frame was locked so the letters couldn't spill out. Then ink was brushed on and paper pressed to it.

These printed pages looked much like the Chinese block pages. But it was easier and quicker to fill frames with type than to carve a story on a block of wood. Johann Gutenberg, a German printer, was one of the first to use movable type.

Printers today fill frames much as those earlier men did. They either set pages by hand or use a typesetter which works like a typewriter. If type falls out of a frame and gets all mixed up we call that a "printer's pie."

Sometimes printers use hand presses. But books, magazines and newspapers are now printed by large electric presses.

When men began to make books, even before the first days of printing, they built libraries in which to keep the books. Those first books were so expensive that they were fastened to the shelves by chains. So of course you didn't need a library card, for you couldn't take any books home! Now every city and almost every town in this country has a library.

If you live in the country your public library may be on wheels. Busses or trailers, called bookmobiles, travel where there are no libraries. You keep the books until the bookmobile comes again.

In school and public libraries, books are arranged so they can be easily found. In your library, do you know where the shelves are that hold the following books?

Picture books. These have many pictures or illustrations.
Fiction. These are make-believe stories.
Non-fiction. You'll find books on how to make things and
about hobbies. Stories of true adventure are here too.

Some other kinds of non-fiction books are:

Poetry. Some books are by one writer, while others have poems by many poets.

Biography. Here you'll find the lives of real people.

Dictionaries. Use these for looking up the spelling of a word as well as its meaning.

Encyclopedias. You can find out about almost anything in the world here.

Atlas. This kind of book has maps and interesting facts about countries.

It's nice to have your own library at home too. It can be part of the family bookcase, or a shelf in your bedroom. Tack these labels on the top edge of the shelf so you can keep your books in their right places: PICTURE BOOKS; FICTION; POETRY; OTHER NON-FICTION; BIOGRAPHY.

There are no finer friends than books. Be sure and use your library card often.

Maps developed along with books as an important means of communication. As people found better ways of communicating they needed better roads over which to send messengers. Good roads meant more travel by foot, horseback and stagecoach.

At this same time there was much more traveling by water. People who had believed the world was flat began to think it was round. So sailors dared to sail farther from shore looking for new routes and countries.

To help people travel on land, maps were needed. Charts, which are water maps, were made to help them travel by ship.

The first maps were drawn or printed on cloth. Even today some cloth maps are made. They can be rolled and don't tear easily. The first charts for sailors were made on papyrus and parchment. Today all ships and even small boats use charts.

We read maps just as people did earlier. The top of the map is always North, the bottom South, the right side East and the left side West.

Every map has a key in one corner. There you'll find a list of the signs used on the map and what they mean. Also, there's a line that tells how long a mile is on the map. This helps you to measure distances.

On an automobile road map, what signs stand for the following: mountains, lakes, railroads, main highways, large cities, airports? What other signs are used?

It's fun to make a map of your neighborhood. If your town is small you can make a map of all of it.

Pretend you're in an airplane looking down. Draw the streets very lightly at first, then put in houses and buildings. On the next page are two different ways it can be done.

Map 1 must have a key in one corner. After each number write what building it stands for. Map 2 is better if done on a very large piece of paper and in color.

Have you ever seen a weather map? If not, write to your nearest United States Weather Bureau for one. You'll see why these maps are important to sailors who want to know when bad storms are coming.

Add maps and charts to your list of ways of communication, for they're important ones. Without them our country might not have been discovered and settled until many years later.

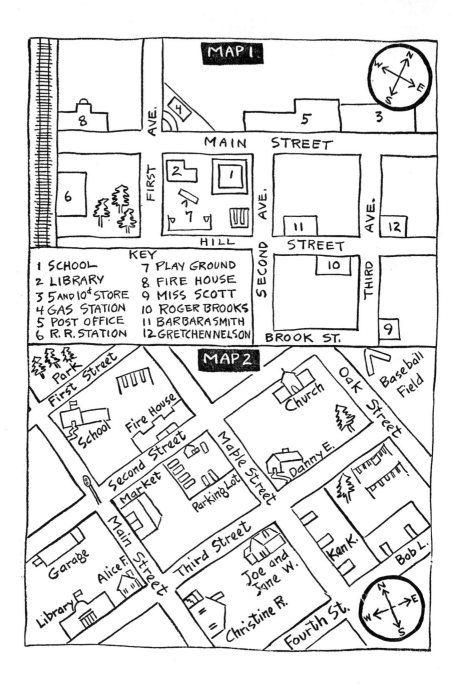

MAP 1

8

4

5

3

MAIN STREET

FIRST AVE.

2

1

6

7

SECOND AVE.

11

THIRD AVE.

12

HILL STREET

10

9

KEY

1 SCHOOL
2 LIBRARY
3 5 AND 10¢ STORE
4 GAS STATION
5 POST OFFICE
6 R. R. STATION
7 PLAY GROUND
8 FIRE HOUSE
9 MISS SCOTT
10 ROGER BROOKS
11 BARBARA SMITH
12 GRETCHEN NELSON

BROOK ST.

MAP 2

Park

First Street

School

Fire House

Second Street

Market

Parking Lot

Maple Street

Church

Oak Street

Baseball Field

Danny E.

Ken K.

Bob L.

Garage

Main Street

Alice F.

Library

Third Street

Joe and Jane W.

Christine R.

Fourth St.

CHAPTER FOUR

When Our Country Was New

THE FIRST people to settle this country, a little over three hundred years ago, brought paper and quill pens with them. They were used to sending letters by mail. For back in England mail was being sent from city to city.

Remember those early runners who carried the first messages and letters? And later, the men who rode horseback and in chariots? They were the first postmen. But they only carried letters for kings and rulers. Other people had to hire a messenger or send a letter by a friend who was traveling.

But at the time our country was being settled, England had horseback riders called postboys who carried mail for everyone. As each rider galloped into a village he blew a loud horn for people to come and get their letters.

The early roads in America weren't good enough for postboys, or postriders as they were later called, so letters were often sent by peddlers who went about the country on foot and horseback. They left the mail in each town's general store, or on a table at an inn. As people stopped by they could pick up their letters. This meant that many letters were months on their way and some of them were lost.

At that time there were no envelopes. Letters were folded with their ends tucked under. Then they were sealed with a small piece of sealing wax. The person receiving the letter paid the postage!

Since letters were often opened along the way it was foolish to send money in them. Instead, people would tear a piece of paper money in half. One part was sent in a letter to a friend. Some days later the other part of the bill was sent in another letter. When the friend pasted the two halves together the money could be used.

After better roads were built postriders carried the mail.

Letters were also sent by stagecoach. The driver kept the mail pouch on the seat beside him so it would be safe.

Stagecoach   Peddler

When California was first settled it took many weeks for mail to get there. So the Pony Express was formed to carry letters from St. Joseph, Missouri, to Sacramento, California. There were eighty riders and they worked much like those early relay riders. A man, with the mail pouch

55

strapped to his saddle, would start off at top speed. He'd gallop to the next relay station, about ten miles along the road. There he'd leap off his horse, throw the mail pouch on a fresh horse and be off again. Every hundred miles a new rider would take over. Since this was wild country each man carried two guns and a knife. But dangerous as it was, only one mail pouch was ever lost by the Pony Express.

The first postmen to deliver to houses carried whistles. They blew these after leaving letters. Today the mailman sometimes rings your bell. But usually he just leaves the mail in your box or by your front door.

If you live in the country you have Rural Free Delivery. This is shortened to R.F.D., or to R.D. A number is written after the letters to tell the postman on which road you live. A country mailbox is on a post beside the road so the mailman can reach it from his car. You know when he has left a letter because the little arm or flag attached to the box will be standing up.

The city postman wears a blue-gray uniform. He delivers

by foot or in a mail truck. On some postmen's coat sleeves you'll see black, red, silver, or gold stars. These tell how many years he has worked. A man wearing three gold stars has carried the mail for forty-five years!

Country or small-town mailmen don't wear uniforms. They deliver by car. In some mountain sections mail is delivered by horseback in summer and by sleigh in winter.

Postmen in other countries of the world dress differently. Some deliver letters in ways we're not used to.

In England you'll often see the mailman riding a bicycle. In some parts of Holland mail is delivered by boat.

If you were an African boy living in a tent in the desert you'd probably get your letters by camel. In other parts of Africa an automobile with very wide tires is used. These keep the car from sinking into the sand.

Both Alaska and Switzerland have long, snowy winters. So mail bags are carried by dog sled in Alaska. While in Switzerland letters are often delivered by mailmen on skis.

Through some of the mountain sections of Pakistan runners carry the mail in relays as those early runners did.

They wear white coats and red turbans, and they carry spears with little bells which tinkle. This warns others coming toward them on the narrow, winding path. Also it may frighten off wild animals.

On page 59 are some of the postmen we've been talking about. In which country might you see them?

You might like to decorate your wall with a large picture called a mural. It could show how the mail was carried from the early days up to now. Or it might be today's mailmen in different parts of the world.

A mural can be painted on a roll of white shelf paper. Or it can be made as the scroll was, by pasting pieces of paper side by side with their edges overlapping. Use drawing paper for a narrow mural and poster paper for a wide one.

Tack this long strip on the wall or spread it on the floor. Draw your pictures lightly in pencil, then color them. Or, if you wish, you can use crayons or paints from the beginning. If your class at school paints a mural, each child will do one part of the picture.

Ask your librarian for other books that tell how the mail was carried. Look in the encyclopedia under Post Office for more pictures.

Now, let's follow a valentine or letter to a friend in a far-off city in this country.

First, the envelope must be addressed carefully so you can be sure your friend will receive it. *Always* put your name and address in the top left corner, or on the back. Then your letter will be returned to you if you've forgotten to put a stamp on it, or if your friend's address is wrong or has been erased. See the envelope on page 61.

If your name and address aren't on the envelope and the letter doesn't get to your friend it will be sent to the "dead-letter office."

When the envelope is sealed and a three-cent stamp pasted on, it's ready for the mailbox. You can read on the outside of the box when the next pick-up is. Remember that A.M. means morning and P.M. is afternoon.

The mailman unlocks the box and your letter rides in his bag to the post office. There it is postmarked. This postmark tells four things:

the name of the town or city

the state it's in

the date

the time

See if you can read the two postmarks below.

POSTMARKS

The postmark, or lines beside it, will cover your stamp so that it can't be used again.

Pin interesting postmarks that come to your house on your bulletin board, or fill a scrapbook with them, arranging them by state and country.

In a small post office the clerk postmarks with a hand stamp. City post offices use canceling machines that can do 500 letters a minute, or 30,000 letters an hour.

Now the letters are sorted and yours is tossed into a pouch that goes to the post office nearest your friend's house. It will be taken there by truck, train, ship, or plane.

At that post office another clerk tosses it into the bag of the postman who delivers on your friend's street or road.

You know that a sealed letter takes a three-cent stamp. What does a postcard need?

To have your letter delivered quickly put a Special Delivery stamp which costs twenty cents beside your three-cent stamp. Letters sent by plane in this country must have a six-cent airmail stamp, or six cents in regular stamps.

Remember how money was torn and sent half at a time during the early days of mail? Now we can send money safely by postal money order.

You'll find a money order slip at the desk in the post office. Fill in these three things: how much money you're sending; your friend's name and address; and at the bottom, your name and address. When you give this slip and the money to the clerk he'll give you a green card. On it will be the same three things you wrote on the slip.

Tear off the right end and keep that. Mail the other end to your friend. He can cash the green money order at any post office or bank. Since no money goes in the envelope no one can steal it.

Every post office, even the small ones that are part of a store or railroad station, has a postmaster. What is a woman in charge of a post office called?

The head of all the post offices in this country is known as the postmaster general. The most important postmaster general during the early days of this country was Benjamin Franklin. He ordered postriders to ride at night as well as during the day. This speeded the mail.

If you or your class visit the back rooms of a post office you'll see many interesting things. Take a list of questions you want the postmaster to answer. Here are some you might like to ask:

1. What is first-class mail? Second-class mail? Fourth-class mail?

2. How many miles might a mailman walk each day?

3. What is the most money you can send by money order?

4. What does it mean to insure a package?

5. What arrangement can business firms make so that their letters do not have to be stamped?

6. What happens to a letter at the "dead-letter office"?

There are two kinds of "post offices on wheels." You may have seen one attached to a passenger train with this sign on it:

UNITED STATES MAIL

RAILWAY POST OFFICE

Inside this car is a small post office. There are sorting desks, big mail pouches, and canceling machines. Clerks work while the train is speeding along.

Mail bags are picked up at the stations where the train stops. Other stations, where the train does not stop, have "mail cranes" beside the tracks. Two steel arms on a post hold a sack of mail. As the train rushes by a steel hook on the mail car reaches out and grabs the bag.

The other moving post office is a large bus or truck with these words on it: UNITED STATES HIGHWAY POST OFFICE. Clerks sort and postmark the mail as the automobile rolls along.

You know about planes that carry mail all over the world. But have you seen a mail helicopter? This is used in large cities to carry letters to airports and nearby cities. Helicopters don't need runways as they can land on the post office roof or in its yard.

Letter writing is something you should learn to do well, for you'll write personal and business letters all your life.

When asking for information be sure you know just what you want to find out. Enclose a three-cent stamp for the return envelope.

One of the most important letters is the "thank you" letter. It's easy because it's short. But don't forget to write it!

If the "thank you" letter is for a present you've received, talk about your gift and how you'll use it. If it's for a visit at someone's house tell what you enjoyed most. Here's a good jingle to remember:

Send "thank you" notes upon their ways
In three sentences, and within three days!

Letters are a fine way of getting to know strangers. You or your class can write to children living in another part of the country or in another country altogether. Tell about your town. If you've made a map of your neighborhood you might like to send that with other pictures. Ask questions about their school and town.

Write a letter to the superintendent of schools in a city in this country, telling him what grade your letter is for. He will tell you where to send your letter. If writing to a foreign country, write first to the mayor of the town you choose. If English isn't spoken in that country find someone in your town to translate the letter. Be sure you put on the right postage for a foreign country.

During those early days of our country another important way of communication came to be used. This was the newspaper.

The Chinese were the first to develop one, for they had a daily paper in Peking, all copied by hand, long before Christ was born.

But the rest of the world was much, much slower. The Romans tacked up news items on a bulletin board in the public square. It was like your school bulletin board, and people stopped to read it on their way by.

When our country was new many villages had a town crier. He walked about ringing a bell and calling out the news. Then several newspapers were started. They were small, weekly papers having only two or four pages, not much like our modern newspapers.

The great newspaper presses of today are wonderful to watch. You'll see how blank paper runs in one end and comes out the other end with its pages printed and in order. Also each newspaper has been automatically folded and counted.

You know how long a minute is. In that time, one mammoth press in New York City can print 1,000 eighty-page newspapers. That makes 60,000 papers an hour!

It's fun to have a home, neighborhood or class newspaper. Before starting one, study different papers. Clip for your bulletin board such departments as: lost and found, book reviews, movie programs, ads. You may want these departments in your paper also: jokes, pets, trips, hobbies, poems, and comics.

Find samples of the following for your bulletin board:

MASTHEAD. This is usually on an inside page. It tells the name of the editor, the paper's address, the date, and the price. It may look like this:

THE WEEKLY NEWS

John Kerr, editor

10 Main St.   Salina, Kan.

Single copy 5¢   Oct. 5, 1953

HEADLINES. These tell what each story is about. Since headlines are to get people to read the story they must be short and interesting. Notice the big type they're printed in.

CAPTIONS. You'll find these under pictures. They tell who's in the picture or what it's about.

If you're running the newspaper alone or with a helper or two you'll be the editor. Your helpers will be reporters. It's their job to find interesting things for the paper.

A class or school newspaper has a larger staff. Then the head of the paper is called the editor-in-chief. Each department has its own editor and several reporters. They write the stories for their part of the newspaper.

The one who arranges the material to be printed in columns is called make-up editor. The proofreader is the person who reads to see there are no mistakes in spelling, grammar and punctuation.

Some of you can write headlines and captions. Others can print or type the paper. Still others on the staff can sell ads, draw pictures, or plan how to distribute the papers.

Writing a news story is different from writing a make-believe story. In a news story the first paragraph tells you, as briefly as possible, five W's. These are: WHO the story is about; WHERE it took place; WHEN it happened; WHAT happened; and WHY it happened. Then, in the following paragraphs, the news writer tells the story in more detail.

Before writing your first news story study several from the front page of a newspaper. Find the five W's. Sometimes you'll find "WHY it happened" has been left out because the reporter doesn't know. Or it might be left until the end of the story, if it is a surprise.

Today we are so used to sending and receiving mail, and to reading newspapers, that we forget how many years it took for both to develop. Ask your librarian for more stories about each of these important ways of communication.

CHAPTER FIVE

Inventions of the Last Hundred Years

THERE are two things that don't sound like communica tion. But without them we'd have no telephones, movies, telegrams, cables, radio or television. These are electricity and the magnet.

Neither of them is new. Electricity was here when Mr. Caveman lived. But since no one could see it, no one knew about it.

However, people through the years noticed certain things that you may have noticed too. Have you ever shuffled across a carpet and touched a person or something made of metal? If so, you've received a "shock" as a small spark jumped from your finger.

Or, perhaps you've combed your hair many times, then held the comb near a piece of paper. You've seen the paper stick to the comb. A glass rod rubbed by a silk cloth also picks up paper.

Such things as these made men curious to know why they happened. So experiments were made.

It was during the early days of our country that many important things about electricity were discovered. Benjamin Franklin, the same man who was our postmaster general, found out that lightning is electricity. You'll enjoy reading the exciting story about his kite experiment in the encyclopedia and in other books.

The magnet was here also when the cavemen lived. Have you ever picked up nails and needles with a small iron magnet? Or rubbed a knife or scissors with a magnet until tacks would stick to them? People through the years noticed these things but thought they were magic. In the early days of our country men found out ways in which the magnet could be used.

The last hundred years have brought the most wonderful

ways of communication the world has ever seen. Yet everything needed to make all of them was here in the beginning. Then why didn't cavemen have radios and telephones? They didn't, because mankind took a long time growing up.

As a baby you were interested mostly in eating and sleeping. So was Mr. Caveman. But also he had to find a home, make the clothes he wore, and hunt for his food. This kept him very busy.

As life became easier, people had more time for experiments. But most men were content to use the things they already knew about. Even if someone discovered something new people weren't interested at first.

Then, transportation was very poor. Men in different parts of the world didn't know what other men had discovered. Also, it was hard to get all kinds of materials. The dial phone of today has four hundred thirty-three parts in it. Materials for these parts must come from many different countries, and without good transportation it would be impossible to gather them.

But slowly, slowly mankind grew up. Transportation became better and faster. Men found many ways to use electricity.

Someone discovered an electric current could be sent through copper wire. Someone else wound copper wire around an iron magnet, making an electromagnet. This was an important discovery. For now an electric current through a wire could be stopped, then started again. It meant that messages could be tapped out in dots and dashes.

Inventions, such as the radio and telephone, are like jigsaw puzzles. If you have all the parts you can put them together. Men, using things discovered in the past, fitted them into something new. Then after each invention, other men tried to improve it.

Such a man was Samuel Morse, who a little over a hundred years ago made the first telegraph set that worked well. Others had made sets, but messages couldn't be heard far off. First of all, Mr. Morse made up a code of dots and dashes. We still use his Morse code which you can see on page 112. Then he built a machine with an electromagnet in it, so he could tap out his words. Finally he found a way to send messages over wires for several miles.

But many people thought this was just a toy. Eight years went by before the first telegraph wire was put on poles between Washington and Baltimore, a distance of forty miles.

At first only one message at a time could be sent over a wire. So people had to wait their turns in sending telegrams. Today, Western Union can send twenty messages over a wire at one time.

Let's see how you can telegraph a friend in another city. First you must plan your telegram carefully, for after the first fifteen words each word costs extra. Little words such as "the," "and," "a" and "I" can be left out. But be sure your message is clear.

Then you can phone your message to Western Union, or you can go to their nearest office and write your words on a telegram blank.

When the telegraph operator gets your message she

types it on a teleprinter. This machine looks like a typewriter but its keys don't make letters. Instead, they punch holes into a narrow moving paper tape. Each letter of the alphabet has so many holes, placed in a certain way. Here's a message sent by hole, or perforated, tape.

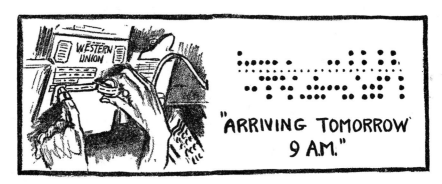

This teleprinter is connected by wire with a machine in another city. The message goes over the wire to that machine, which types the words on another moving paper tape. The operator there cuts off the message and pastes it on a telegram form as shown in the picture.

Now it's ready for a Western Union messenger to deliver to your friend. Sometimes the message is read to him over the phone.

76

If you visit a telegraph office the operator might let you have a piece of perforated tape for your bulletin board. Ask her what happens if their messenger can't find your friend's house. Also, ask her how long it takes for a message of fifteen words to go across the country.

Here's a telegram game that's fun to play. Choose a word of seven to ten letters such as *writings, mammoth, printers* or *delivered.* Plan a message with each letter starting a word. If you choose *writings* you might say, "William Root is telephoning in Newton's general store." Or for *mammoth* you could write, "Mother and Mary met on the hill."

If you'd like to make a telegraph set with batteries ask your librarian for a book that tells how.

You see telegraph poles and wires in towns and all through the countryside. Have you noticed the glass cups the wires pass through? Electricity likes to run away. If it weren't for those glass cups the electricity in the wire would run down the pole into the ground. Then, of course, no messages could be sent.

Cities put their wires underground. Otherwise there'd

be so many telegraph, telephone and electric light wires that streets would look like spider webs.

Remember how money is sent by postal money order? You can send it quicker by telegraph money order. Just fill out the blank at the Western Union office, telling the same three things you did for your postal money order. Then give the clerk the money you're sending. As soon as your friend receives the telegram he can collect the money at his telegraph office.

Soon after it was found that the telegraph really worked, it was planned to run wires under water too. Such wires are called submarine cables, or just cables. At first these cables were not successful, for the covering of tar and rubber used on the wires soon wore out. Besides, the electricity ran away into the water.

Then the part needed for that puzzle was found! Men had been working with something you'll enjoy saying, gutta-percha. This milky gum is from a tree. It becomes hard when dry. Some golf balls and knife handles are made of it. Gutta-percha is a fine covering for cables as it wears well and it won't let the electricity escape.

It was hard work laying the first submarine cable under the Atlantic Ocean. The bottom of the ocean is much like land. Some parts are flat and other parts are hilly and mountainous. When these mountains stick above water, we call them islands. So the easiest and best way across the ocean bottom had to be found. Finally the first successful cable from our country to England was laid in 1866. How thrilled people were with those early messages!

There are many things that still bother submarine cables such as big fish, ships' anchors, and bad storms. Many cable ships are kept busy laying new cables and repairing old ones.

You can send a cablegram now to any country in the world. But you must plan a very short message, for this costs more than a telegram.

One man who was very much interested in the telegraph was a teacher of deaf children, Alexander Graham Bell. He believed that the voice, as well as dots and dashes, could be sent along wires. So he made a machine that was to be our first telephone.

You know how waves roll out from a stone that's been

79

dropped into calm water. Sound waves do the very same thing. Whenever anyone speaks, sound waves go out into the air.

These sounds make nearby things move, but such a tiny bit you can't see it. However, if you turn your radio on as loud as it will go you can prove this. Dishes and windows will rattle.

Inside everyone's ear is an eardrum. This moves too when sound hits it.

Mr. Bell knew these things. So he made a mouthpiece with a kind of eardrum in it called a diaphragm. This diaphragm was fixed to move whenever anyone spoke near it. Fastened to it were wires and an electromagnet. At the other end of the wires was another mouthpiece. After many, many tries Mr. Bell was able to send his voice over the wire.

The first telephones had no receivers, only the mouthpiece. You spoke into the mouthpiece, then quickly held it to your ear to listen for the reply.

The diaphragms in the early mouthpieces didn't move

as easily as they do now. So one had to shout in order to make the person at the other end hear.

Today's mouthpiece is like an electric ear, with a thin, steel diaphragm for its eardrum. It is no longer necessary to shout.

The first telephone operators in this country were young boys. They ran about helping each other make connections. But they were so noisy and took so long that women were trained for this work instead.

Have you noticed what pleasant voices women operators have? And how polite they are?

A small town needs only one telephone operator, for it has only one switchboard. A large city has a number of telephone offices, called exchanges, with many operators at each exchange.

Every operator has her own switchboard to watch. She wears earphones so her hands will be free.

This is what happens when you use a manual phone. As you lift the receiver a light flashes above your number on a switchboard at the telephone office. The operator sees this light and pulls up a long, wire cord which has a metal end. She plugs this end into the hole by your number. This connects her with you, and she says, "Number please."

When you've told her, she pulls up another cord and plugs it into the hole by that number. Your friend's phone rings. As soon as he picks up his receiver you're connected with him.

When you hang up, the light by your number flashes again. This tells the operator you're through talking. So she pulls out both cords.

A dial phone works like this. First you pick up your receiver and let the phone talk to you. It will say, "Mmmm." This means "Number please." Now, dial your numbers carefully, waiting for a click after each number. You'll be connected with your friend by an electrical machine at the telephone exchange.

Here are some good telephone rules to remember: keep your lips one half inch from the mouthpiece; speak in your normal voice; answer the phone as soon as you hear it ringing; be sure the number you call is right. Can you think of other phone rules?

When you visit a telephone office here are some questions you might like to ask:

1. Why am I sometimes cut off when talking to a friend?
2. When that happens what should I do?
3. If I can't find a number in the phone book who can help me?
4. How can I call long-distance on a dial phone?
5. If my phone is out-of-order what should I do?

Two play telephones you can really use are easy to make. See how on pages 106 and 108.

Today we can telephone to people on trains, airplanes, ships and even in automobiles. But as you know these phones don't have wires like home phones have. So before such telephones were possible there had to be another great invention. This was the wireless.

In Italy lived a man named Guglielmo Marconi. He tried to send sound waves without wires. For this he built two towers. Each had an antenna on top. One tower was for sending messages by Morse code, the other for receiving them. After many, many experiments Mr. Marconi was able to send a message of dots and dashes from one tower to the other.

Many men tried to improve this wonderful invention. Some thought that since sounds could be carried through the air without wires, perhaps voices could be too. At last Lee De Forest, who is called the father of radio and television, found out how to send music through the air. Then it was discovered that voices could be sent from one station to another. Now the wireless is usually called the radio!

Today by radio we hear news from all over the world right after it happens. Messages sent to ships are called radiograms. Airports use radio beams to guide pilots in during fogs or bad storms.

Police cars and many taxicabs have two-way radios on which they can both send and receive messages. A walkie-talkie is a small two-way radio that can be carried easily. You can talk to people a few miles away with it. An even smaller two-way radio is the handie-talkie which is used by paratroopers.

Perhaps you've seen one of these words under a newspaper picture: *Wirephoto* or *Radiofoto*. These tell you that the photograph was sent by wireless.

But we couldn't have Wirephotos or photos of any kind except for another great invention, the camera. Not much more than one hundred years ago, if you wanted a picture of yourself you had to hire an artist to draw or paint it. This was expensive, so very few people could afford it.

Then came the first cameras—large, strange-looking machines. Photographs were printed on copper. Later, tin was used and those pictures were called tintypes.

In those days a person had to sit still from three to thirty minutes to have a picture taken. So an iron stand was placed behind his chair. This had clamps which fastened to his head to keep it from moving. When you see these early tintypes you'll laugh at how stiff people look.

Cameras have three important parts: a finder, lens and shutter. You look through the finder to see the picture you're taking. The lens is a piece of glass at the front of the camera. It opens when you move the shutter. Light from the picture you're taking flashes through this tiny opening and hits the film inside the camera. Chemicals on the film break down where the light touches and thus the photograph is formed. It will be upside down on the film.

You can make a pinhole camera that will show how the picture looks inside a real camera. Find out how on page 109.

If you have a camera, learn to take good pictures. Remember these camera rules:

1. Plan your picture carefully. Look at it through the finder.
2. See that there are darks and lights in your picture, for these make it more interesting.
3. Put your camera on something solid so it won't move as you snap the picture. Or hold your breath as you take it.
4. Look into the finder, not at your picture, as you push the shutter.
5. Turn to the next film right away, so you won't use one film twice. For that would be a double exposure, which is one picture on top of another.

Some children develop their own films. If you have a grownup to help you, ask the librarian for a good book on film developing.

Your class at school will enjoy a photograph contest. Let class members bring only pictures they've taken themselves. These can be portraits (pictures of people), landscapes (pictures of scenery), seascapes (pictures of the sea and shore). Also, there can be photographs of pets, buildings, and other interesting things. Ask three grownups to be judges.

About the time the camera was becoming popular another kind of communication came into use. This was the typewriter.

It didn't look much like the typewriter of today, and it printed only capital letters. But it was a wonderful invention. For until then all stories, books, letters, plays, poems—everything—had to be written by hand.

Now many schools have typewriters for pupils in the lower grades to use. They're a great help if you have trouble with spelling. For you'll remember a word better after you've typed it several times.

COMMUNICATION

How different our world would be today without the many great inventions of the last one hundred years. It's hard for us to imagine how people got along before the telegraph, cable, telephone, wireless, radio, camera and typewriter.

CHAPTER SIX

New Ways of Talking and Listening

MANY, MANY YEARS ago there was a kind of moving picture. Egyptian children had a toy that looked like a large spool. All around the spool were slits, cut close together. In each slit was a small card with a slightly different picture on it. These cards might have looked like the pictures on page 90.

By turning the spool and flipping the edges of the cards it would look as if the man were lifting the stone.

Today's animated cartoons that you see in the movies are made much the same way. Many pictures are drawn by artists. Then a camera takes photographs of all these pictures in order. When the film is shown, the characters look as if they're really moving. A five-minute animated

cartoon needs several thousand different drawings.

Another kind of moving picture was made on an Egyptian scroll. You might like to write a play and show it as these early children did. First, make a long scroll like the one told about on page 39. Divide it into the number of scenes you need, each about one or two feet wide.

For *Jack and the Beanstalk* you might start with the scenes shown on the opposite page.

90

When giving your play ask another child to help you. As you *slowly* unroll one side he can roll the other. The play can be shown silently, or you may tell the story as it's unrolled. Or you and your friend can talk for the characters.

Motion pictures of today were made possible by many inventions. Two of the important ones were the work of a great American, Thomas Edison. He built a machine for taking pictures on film. These made much better photographs than tintypes.

Also, he made the first phonograph which he called a "talking machine." We couldn't have talking pictures without this. The first talking pictures had records that played while the film was being shown. Today, the sound track is part of the film.

To make a record a person speaks or sings into a tube. This is connected to a cutting tool that moves whenever sound hits it. Under this tool is a soft wax record with grooves cut in it. The point of the tool follows the grooves, making little marks from side to side as the sound vibrations come through the tube.

When you buy a copy of this record your phonograph needle will follow these markings. Then the sounds will be played back to you.

Radio stations often use recordings of music, speeches and commercials instead of "live" programs. Records called "talking books" are made for blind people, so they can hear books other people enjoy reading.

There are recording machines that use wire or tape instead of records. Some schools have these recorders to help students learn to speak better. Pupils talk into a tube, then they listen to their own voices as the wire or tape is played back.

Another recorder is the dictaphone, a machine used mostly in business offices. In answering letters, a man speaks his answers into the tube of the dictaphone. As he does so a record, the shape of a tin can, is made. Later, a typist listens to this record and types the letters as she hears them.

Two inventions important to all of us are the radio and

television. You remember in the last chapter we learned that the wireless and radio are the same thing—sound waves sent through the air. Mr. Marconi used two towers with which to send and receive messages. Today, the broadcasting building is the sending station and your radio is the receiving station.

Inside a radio you'll see glass tubes that light up when the set is turned on. These are called vacuum tubes and they're very important. For when your antenna catches a program, these tubes make it loud enough to be heard. Lee De Forest, the man who sent music through the air, was the one who perfected the radio tube.

Radio waves go easily around the world. But television waves stop whenever they hit something high such as a mountain. Or when they come to where the earth curves they run away into the air. So high relay towers have been built to catch the television waves and send them on to the next tower. Watch for these relay towers. You will see many of them across the countryside.

Television waves are also sent by coaxial cable. This is

94

a brass-covered cable, filled with wires, that runs under the ground.

Broadcasting stations are interesting to visit. The rooms where programs are put on must be soundproof. Do you know why?

The singer or speaker on a radio program stands in front of a microphone, or mike, as it is called. This has a mouthpiece that picks up sounds. On a television program you don't often see the mikes, but several are hidden about the room.

Television plays are given in large rooms called studios. In different parts of the room you'll see scenery for each act. Props (the chairs, tables, telephones, and other things needed in a play) are all in place before the program begins. So the actors just move from one scene to the next, with the cameras following.

The sound man has an interesting job. He must be ready to make every sound in the play as it's needed.

There are three kinds of sound effects: real, imitated and recorded. Real sounds are door and telephone bells, and other small things easy to keep in a studio.

But many sounds must be imitated. To make you think bacon is frying the sound man crumples cellophane paper. A long sheet of metal hanging in a doorway makes wonderful thunder when it is touched.

In cowboy plays the sound of horses must be imitated. Tapping first one rubber sink plunger and then another on a table makes you think a horse is walking on pavement. If the horse is galloping along a gravel road the sound man can use two halves of a cocoanut, pounding one and then the other very fast on the table.

Try these and other sound effects of your own. Let your family guess what you are imitating.

Then there are noises the sound man can't bring into the studio or imitate. He plays records of such things as a rooster crowing, dogs barking, a train leaving a station, and a baby crying.

In television plays, three or more cameras follow the actors about. The pictures taken by each camera are flashed to screens in a control room. There the director decides which picture is best and that is the one sent over the air.

Plan a radio program for your family. Or have your class give a program for another class. You can make a play microphone. Fasten it to a broomstick which is nailed onto a board so the mike will stand alone.

A variety program is interesting. This can include a news broadcast, a play, the reading of a short story or several poems, and music. Be sure to rehearse the program until it runs smoothly.

Have you ever seen a television truck? It carries cameras, microphones, and a crew of two or three men. These trucks go to football and baseball games, outdoor meetings and to other places of interest. They make it possible for you to see many programs that are taking place outside the studio.

Drivers of television trucks, as well as drivers of all cars, know another kind of communication. It's important to bicycle riders too. This is communication by traffic signs.

Some highway signs tell you about the road ahead. What do these say to you?

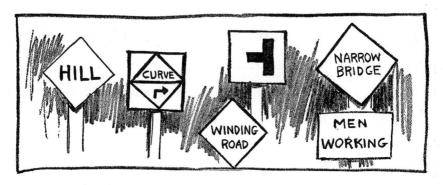

Some traffic signs tell you what you can't do. What do these NO signs say?

Still other signs tell you how to drive safely. M.P.H. stands for Miles Per Hour. What do these signs mean?

Watch for still different highway and traffic signs both in town and on the highways. Decide what they are saying to YOU.

There are other communication signs you'll see when traveling. These are posters, and their big brothers the billboards. Although both are old means of giving messages, they are used today in new and interesting ways.

The first posters were those news items we spoke about in Chapter Four which the Romans nailed to a post or bulletin board. It is from the word "post" that posters and other important communication words came. Can you name the ten words we've talked about that start with "post"? They are listed on page 115 of the index.

Today, posters are made to catch your attention, and to tell you something quickly. Large, simple pictures and bright colors are used to catch your attention. The messages on posters and billboards are short, so you can read them easily as you are walking or riding by.

You'll enjoy drawing posters. They are made for such things as: candy sale, puppet show, class play, photograph contest, Book Week, a sports event.

Remember those five W's used in writing a news story: WHO, WHEN, WHERE, WHAT, and WHY? Be sure and keep them in mind when you are drawing posters.

There are still many more ways of communicating. Some are listed below. The dictionary and encyclopedia will tell you about them.

Ways of telling stories: wampum belt, quipus, totem pole, obelisk, hornbook.

Ways of telling time: sundial, hourglass, clepsydra, curfew.

Ways of signaling: Paul Revere's lanterns, heliograph, cannons, flag semaphore code, train semaphore, train block system.

There are some new and exciting ways of communication coming along. One is colored television which will be in many homes before long. Another is a rocket that is being built to shoot mail across the Atlantic Ocean. Watch for news of them in your newspapers.

There's a new kind of moving picture which is three-dimensional and makes you think the movie is being acted right in the room with you. A radio is planned called Binaural, which means "two ears." This, like the three-dimensional moving picture, will make music and voices seem even more real than now.

When you're grownup, you may think of a still better way of telling or sending messages. You might be the one to invent a new way of communication for the world.

CHAPTER SEVEN

Things to Do

WHEN YOU do and make the things you read about it helps you to understand and remember them. Besides, it's fun!

So far in this book you've learned to do or make the following: clay tablet; wax tablet; your own museum, library shelf and bulletin board; scroll; quill pen; secret ink; flag and flashlight wigwagging; maps of your neighborhood and town; mural; newspaper; early moving picture; radio and television programs; photograph contest; poster.

Here are more things for you to do or make. Be sure and read directions carefully. Get everything you need in one place. Then, take your time.

PARCHMENT

You need:

> piece of rabbit skin, sheepskin, or kidskin
> large, old pan
> rubber gloves
> knife
> board
> thumbtacks
> from drugstore: bottle of limewater
> can of powdered pumice
> from art store: can of white French chalk

Directions:

Wearing rubber gloves, pour the limewater into the old pan. Push the skin into it until well covered. Let this soak for three days, or until the hair on the skin is loose.

Put on the rubber gloves and take the skin from the lime-water. Stretch it and thumbtack it to the board. While it is wet, pull and scrape with the knife until all the hair is off. Now, wash the skin well with clear water and let it dry on the board for several hours.

To make it smooth, rub the skin well with powdered pumice and dust it with the French chalk. Or mix the pumice and chalk, half and half, with a little water. Using a cloth, rub the skin with this.

When the parchment is smooth, cut it into sheets the size of a page. You may use ink on it, but be sure to *print* your words.

BLOCK PRINTING

The Chinese used wood for making block prints. But this is hard to cut, so we'll use linoleum instead. It prints on paper just as those early wood blocks did, and many copies may be made from each linoleum block.

Designs and initials can be used on bookmarks, book plates and stationery. For book covers and gift wrapping paper, stamp many small designs on a piece of paper. Scenes are good for Christmas cards and valentines.

You need:

piece of linoleum at least ¼ inch thick. Use new linoleum that bends easily without cracking.

block of wood the size of linoleum

water color paint or printer's ink. If oil paint is used, put it on with a roller.

small paint brush

piece of transparent paper

piece of carbon paper

drawing or writing paper on which to print pictures

tools—gouging tools from an art store. Or make your own from old umbrella spokes cut three inches long. Insert each into a handle made from a broomstick cut into three-inch pieces. File ends of spokes until sharp.

Directions:

Glue your linoleum to the block of wood.

Draw your design or picture on the transparent paper. If you use words, put the letters close together and draw each one with a double line.

Now, place the carbon paper *face down* on the linoleum. Put your design on top of that *face down* also. Trace it carefully.

Remove the two papers. Hold your linoleum in front of a mirror to see how it will look when printed. The letters will face the right way in the mirror if you've traced your picture *face down*.

Cut out the background of your picture. Dig in about ⅛ inch. If you want your letters to print white cut out between their double lines. For black letters, cut out the space around them.

Paint all the raised parts of the design with your paints or printer's ink.

Now, place the paper on which you wish to print on top of the linoleum. *Never* let the paper move once it's been put on the block. Press the paper with your hand or with a rolling pin. Or put it on the floor with a piece of tin or wood covering it and stand on it with one foot.

Put your prints where they can dry well.

TIN CAN TELEPHONE

You need:

2 baking powder cans with tops off. Or two soup cans

with one end cut out. File the cut ends until they are very smooth.

2 large nails

1 long piece of fine, single-strand wire

The cans are your mouthpieces. Bore a hole big enough for the wire to go through in the middle of the end of each can. Push the ends of the wire through the holes up into the cans. Fasten there to a nail. Your phone will look like this:

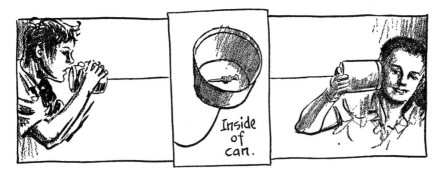

Inside of can.

You and a friend can stand in different rooms. Keep the wire *tight* between you and speak loudly into the can. Use the mouthpiece for both talking and listening, and speak very clearly.

BOX TELEPHONE

You need:

> 2 round salt or oatmeal boxes. Cut out both ends of
> the boxes carefully.
> large piece of heavy wrapping paper
> strong cord
> large needle
> small piece of butter or lard

The boxes are your mouthpieces. Cover one end of each box with wrapping paper. Tie it on the box with cord. Rub the paper lightly with butter or lard.

With the needle, punch a hole in the center of each paper cover big enough for your cord to go through. Run each end of a long piece of cord through these holes and up into the boxes. Tie a large knot in each end so the string can't pull back out.

When talking, keep the string *tight* between you and your friend. Use the mouthpiece for both talking and listening.

REBUS LETTER

PINHOLE CAMERA

This pinhole camera will show you how a picture looks inside a real camera.

You need:

> pasteboard box, such as a shoe box or large cracker box

knife or scissors

piece of wax paper the size of one end of the box

darning needle

adhesive tape about 1 inch wide

Directions:

Cut out one end of the box, leaving a half inch margin all around. Over this end paste the wax paper.

In the center of the box's other end carefully make a hole with the needle. Now, tape all the edges of the box so no light can get in except through the little hole.

Put a dark cloth or coat over your head and part of the camera. Hold the end with the wax paper toward you, about 1 foot from your eyes. Point the hole at a sunny scene. You'll see trees and buildings upside down on the wax paper screen.

THE MORSE CODE

You can send Morse code messages with a drum, whistle, flashlight or flag.

In using a drum or whistle remember that a dot is a short

tap or toot, a dash is a long tap or toot.

If wigwagging by flag or flashlight, read again the directions on page 30. Remember that a dot is signaled to the right, a dash to the left.

After signaling a letter, count to three. After each word, count to five. At the end of every sentence, count to twenty-five. These pauses will help the person who is receiving your message.

There are two good ways to learn the Morse code. They are:

1. Practice the letters in order, three at a time, until you can do them quickly.
2. Learn the alphabet in this order:
   Letters that are all dots: E   I   S   H
   Letters that are all dashes: T   M   O
   Letters that start with a dot: A   W   J   R   L   P
   Letters that start with a dash: N   D   B   K   Y
   X   C
   Rest of letters: U   F   V   G   Q   Z

On the next page you will find the Morse code.

111

Morse Code

(*International*)

A	· —		N	— ·
B	— · · ·		O	— — —
C	— · — ·		P	· — — ·
D	— · ·		Q	— — · —
E	·		R	· — ·
F	· · — ·		S	· · ·
G	— — ·		T	—
H	· · · ·		U	· · —
I	· ·		V	· · · —
J	· — — —		W	· — —
K	— · —		X	— · · —
L	· — · ·		Y	— · — —
M	— —		Z	— — · ·

Index

INDEX